BENDING SPOONS

CHARLIE FOOS

ugly duckling presse
2004

Bending Spoons
isbn # 0-9727684-6-7

Copyrite Charlie Foos 2004

distributed by:
SPD/Small Press Distribution
orders@spdbooks.org
(800) 869-7533

For Bunny,
the King,
& the Queen

I'd take the fire.
-Jean Cocteau

Chapter 1

<u>IRRATIONAL FEAR OF MURDERS</u>

1 I assume
the game of love
erotic as eating meatloaf with their fingers
you know what
I want to be
I'll marry you.

2 Financing up to 48 months
Kari hi
so this is what big kids do
they're hiring down at my job
this is our future
what about your sister.

3 Temperatures drop fast
where do some of America's most successful
people get their start
well
for many people
you know these muscles are working
that's nice.

4   Call for important lease details
        I was mouth'n off to my brother
        take a look at those cars
        everything you can do, it was never enough
        Pat loves pizza
        yahoo, America online.

5   Good shot
        if you've ever had to apply
        there's different levels
        hey I'm ready
        baby's really bad
        desk drawer.

6   Get the job done
        let's get her
        ladies and gentlemen
        five dollars friday after five
        Russell I didn't want to go out with you
        we use our volume buying power
        I just don't believe he did it.

7   Giants fans
        boy this is great
        bombshell
        but you really have developed a reputation
        stronger
        still love inside of me
        online voice messages.

8   Ab Rocker
        25 25
        lower cholesterol
        38 minuets
        afterwards
        1 carat solitaire
        hundreds and hundreds of reps.

9   Rapid results
        sort of tell us
        you want
        very very well
        tonight
        I couldn't stop looking in the mirror.

10   That's the way she is at home
that's what my skill is
four different workouts
new allegations
take care of their bodies
how many different men are you sleeping with.

11   Whenever you want 'em
hey guys
we don't have to worry about
Kelly Hoo
have you gone through that yourself
why don't we go tell them
about my girls on Corvette's calendar.

12   He's kind to animals
a man or a woman
the bowl championship
study of 5,000 women
usually you only hear about the big winners
what a nice surprise
he was trying to stop a tank.

13   Really love their cars
      fast
      all your favorite shows
      28
      he understands Japanese
      what a day for a daydream
      presenting the new Italian originals.

14   Sing
      airlines non-stop
      good french fry
      still no place like it
      could save you 15%
      so is Jen around.

15   Aneurism
      tonight
      no we're not talkin' about the Grand Ole Opry
      group in the middle
      lot o' calls comin' in
      it's that way
      sale of narcotics.

16   It will have America talkin'
        it's your future
        we've had problems in recent weeks
        find a way to get some easy baskets
        take 'em away please
        and Ralph Lauren came in.

17   Really white
        I don't care what it smells like
        it's time for the tax refunds
        I'm not sure why
        he had Jones completely whipped
        for 125,000 dollars
        throw out your old underwear.

18   Beauty is a curse
        I am about to introduce you
        new commercials
        40%
        a Woodrow Wilson
        pay back.

19   Young man
        I look like I had a pretty good time
        in a number of hamburger commercials
        in the middle of your bed
        we'll be right back
        listen to me
        this is a social security measure.

20   I need to run
        the worst case scenario
        being as your husband
        this music makes me want to dance
        I'll go with dinner
        time flies.

21   Money coming out of the wazoo
        risk of a heart attack
        you've got it all
        destroy the ship
        flipped his van
        switched style
        out of the blue.

22   Shot by the police
        o.k.
        master of suspense
        medical condition
        are you a serious man
        then again
        standing by.

23   I'm glad it's over
        phoning here
        this is insane
        been talking with some residents
        that's going to be my wife
        corporal
        the hostages have been taken in the police car.

24   I'm taking the pill
        touch
        step inside
        others include deep wells
        order
        we'll have them to use
        blue skies spring advance.

25   This one is different from the other ones
        I'm spending about two minutes
        I probably won't get this one right
        every year
        I have a twin
        there's so many different ways.

26   I want to be your senator
        fifty-eight
        as you slide forward
        o.k. bachelor number two
        that's my baby
        there you go
        one of the best things you can do.

Chapter 2

POKING THE EYE

1
Buy factor direct
I've heard
this is an amazing time.

2
How can you get one with bad credit
not a great sign
1991.

3
She's alright
tax professionals
and good things happen.

4
Now Elise that's not possible
that makes renting easy
William Hurt.

5

So let's meet them
Saturday at noon
the best deal anywhere.

6

Free tickets
speech, yeah yeah
click light.

7

And you can fold it up
sexy as you
inside or out.

8

Seventy-five fifty-five
another man
call and get yours free.

9
15 years old
bow to the queen
his guest appearance on Oprah.

10
I want you to get an idea of her attitude
you can warm her up
I lost 4 inches off my waist.

11
More than that
we can't let this go on
you know.

12
Ain't nothin' you can do about it
and there's more
here I was at 255 pounds.

13
Girl
and retouched by Shannon
millions of people everywhere.

14
If you live long enough
speaking of lesbians
all new advanced Tae Bo.

15
Eight Tylenol to do that
do you want me to tell you what we know
that's locked in savings.

16
Even if you're in the best of health
when she was a kid
I was in the rodeo ring.

17
If so call
I channel her
I want to lose weight.

18
You keep your mouth shut
we'll be right back
one thing that I thought was really cool.

19
Why you cryin'
I think I'm lost
I don't want to lose that.

20
The piece de resistance
built in massage
I could do that.

21

Jesus the epic mini-series
we'll be doin' something
a tiny miracle.

22

On the monitor
the kids grow up
famous names on the list.

23

Joy has done it for many years
my father
all about survival.

24

57 hours of fear, anxiety, and pain
it ain't that happy a day
calling him the genius.

25
You think I'm too old for you
people will listen
the real heroes are the highway workers.

26
Look at the size of those paws
three people are under arrest
a bizarre sword attack.

27
Going through the rubble
police officers
a flash of steel.

28
He thanks God
newborn infant daughter
it's catastrophic.

29
She got rid of propane
animated and excited
back to you Vick.

30
Defunked
honey please be careful
the safety of people.

31
Flames shooting
national model
explosion.

32
He kicked your butt
I don't think we brought enough stuff
yeah.

33
Waters are the same
let me see what else I can do
I hate you.

34
Roommate wanted
an allergic reaction
people like us.

35
I left that in Philly
let go of my hand
Mark says, Greg's boat turned.

36
A chance to win
there's more
for that matter.

37
Come clean
stories that reveal injustice
he's got it made.

38
The best guarantee
it's all the best thinking
in case you are wondering.

39
Live from the avenue
he leaves crucial
president.

40
Trust me
in the pantry
7 under par.

41
Throw in the towel
about to move on out'a here
shower early.

42
Stickier than it was yesterday
it's the crossroads of American value
it all comes together.

43
Yasir Arafat
July 15th
swims upstream.

44
Pure poetry
our 24 hour tailoring
scientists here.

45
Week nights at seven
thank you very much
jobs lost.

46
World headquarters in New York
brutality charges
get rid of Gretchen right away.

47
I should be the first to go
like he was a dog or something
voting.

48
Don't tell your friends
Philadelphia
using whatever force they need.

49
Monitor the department
caution
Baltimore's favorite.

50
No interest
willing to let go
well it's just the way it is.

51
Big Brother
who ever knew he'd do something like this
you take your son to the doctor.

52
He's tall for his age
it's a nice thing that he did
double the purchase price.

53
The new Michael J. Fox
and all that stuff
for freshness.

54
Even ice cream tastes better
why are you staring at me
spokesperson for the actress.

55
Super quiet
we can work with that
and Monica says.

56
Laughing at his weight
nothing protects more comfortably
this mother of two.

57
An official accident
only on eleven
french fries.

58
Matthew come on out
it's an honor
behind the scenes.

59
Lost souls
is he still mad at me
what is she.

60
Lay it all out
do girls not like funny guys
he didn't approve.

You roll your eyes
as we once were
yes definitely.

The savings are sizzling
it's a long day
to be used in making mattresses.

We learned a lot
you don't even know what you're talking about
you were right.

The gang's all here
don't even go there
twenty-nine bucks.

65
Career opportunity
tell me right now
heart burn relief.

66
Twelve hours later
she got all mad
my next guest.

67
History and Government
sure it doesn't run
Casey wake up.

68
You're getting married
there's summer's eve
left all alone.

69
Ever since she was born
possibility
what was she writing.

70
I'm positive
rhythm abnormalities
determination.

71
The dream so real
I have a question
so do I.

72
Coffee
what's up with it
he was on Broadway.

73

A depressed neighboring nation
only $1.99
keep the hair we've lost.

74

New and improved
please sit
my doctor.

75

I won't let it get me down
absolutely
you're obviously a stickler for clean.

76

Control is everything
the plain truth is
the million man march.

77
Nine European countries
right on
connect.

78
I have spoken
it's real TV
capture here exotic expedition.

79
No sign of a Starbucks
these warriors are wearing skirts
inspect the house.

80
Calm down
for more than sixty years
I miss her.

81
Could it be Big Foot
it wasn't like I planned on that
love has no color.

82
Gorilla jokes
60 days
nice decent white men.

83
Paid for his house arrest
somewhat above partisanship
I am supporting.

84
Reclaiming his community
she's got this other guy
he's back home.

85
Teach me better
searching
to suppress statements.

86
Switching parties
for over twenty years
that's fine.

87
Listening to something we can't hear
every time
you have a lot of new things.

88
I have to be careful
freedom
seven hours before calling.

89
They had to pray
you've got it all
until I moved in.

90
The body you've always wanted
few will not participate
virility.

91
The soul train
with absolutely no increase
make completions.

92
Incomplete
to help get you on your way
the service is free.

93
You gotta let it bump
come in
there's a place.

94
Your name
I'm saying
just as I was leaving.

95
I do anything
truck drivers
just a few more throws.

96
You only meant to crack his head
and taste
this four pack.

97
Really big sheets
yes
we built our house.

98
The best show of the season
did you win
she's a girl.

99
Sexual assault
my man Mike
close by storms.

100
A fence
think of something
how far along are you.

101
Back to back
boulder, richer
hi, my name is Jerry.

102
Not moving at all
is there really such a thing
just in time.

103
I'll close the deal
straight
build your credit faster.

104
Solo shot
things are looking great
it's labor day.

105
Something amazing is about to happen
it's back
this might be a first.

106
Jesus lost
a lot of great information
take a look at the fast work.

107
These people are getting screwed
we'll send you a check
it wasn't even planned.

108
50 thousand dollars to leave
in the field
open your eyes and wake up.

109
Join the NRA now
totally destroyed
that was a hefty bag.

110
Sex with four women at once
you pay for it
we're out of business.

111
You would be better off living in Texas
seemingly harmless
the tonight show band.

112
Without any obligation
people abuse the system
there's no docks.

113
Racers rip it up
calcium
you have to remember.

114
The criminal has the advantage
nothing compares
here's one from Canada.

115
In their native language
firemen
receive a silver-plated bullet with Charlton Heston's signature.

116
Bush
hey guys this isn't funny
some people are always thinking.

117
Brand new president
help you breathe easier
he did what.

118
Such an amazing show
the internet
call Edison.

119
Maybe I should have got the ranch
illegal play
last thing I'll mention.

120
Nude pictures
the late show is starting now
the joke is over, give him his magazine back.

125
Car pool
more flexibility
Brando takes up hang gliding.

126
A hot cup of Joe
shaved back
ask how it feels.

127
Yes to Gore
the time has come for us to say sayonara
forward now.

128
Good taste
doctor says
Jack the skating chimp.

129
Please don't kill me
ten hours a day
trying to make sense of all this.

130
East Baltimore
you were clothed at all times
I will never ask.

131
Really interesting and fun to talk to
it's the tooth fairy
to addiction.

132
Mona Lisa
you didn't
why don't you go next.

133
I was a junkie
in jewel tone colors
you can't beat it.

134
13 million hit a day
some women
I want to protect my family.

135
For eight years
the male anatomy
become a pop singer.

136
You never know when it's going to end
that's great
it's not true.

137
The reality of real life
time to buy
he won so much last time.

138
What are you yellin' for
we gotta go
America again turns to Peter Jennings.

139
You can't get it off
you can't beat it
another chocolate attack.

140
After the controversy
George W. Bush
I've talked to the mothers of Texas.

141
What the American people know
it's just different
start over.

142
What we've done is just phenomenal
the dog's barking
I don't give a damn.

143
Don't listen to him
let's say yes
your life is waiting.

144
Gentlemen
this isn't going to be pretty
you assassinated my character.

145
Giving them final cut
thinking about the sad state of education
that's the media's problem.

146
I'm taking control
seems so trivial
give him 160 mgs.

147
New information released
you shame yourself
with her all the time.

148
No evidence of sexual assault
what do you think
I'm worried she's getting tired of me.

149
What can I do for you
for the latest
I am built to take you anywhere.

150
Wait and see
it was nothing
he's my age.

151
Enjoy the ignorance
only when he's around
you know what time it is.

152
No more barking
seven times a night
know what I mean.

157

Use your credit card
they're tripping around Las Vegas
this feels right.

158

I don't need any of that
vending machine
do you love me.

159

I couldn't sleep at all last night
I'm kind of a fan of pressure points
let me do my job.

160

This is not a dishwasher
it's very fun
an important part of American History.

161
Keep your eyes open boys
recount
we can't move it now.

162
This Friday
you're sitting on Grandpa's knee
that's the whole idea.

163
20 days on distilled water
in the East River
you did this on purpose.

164
The wedding is off
see inside
that's a lot of eggs.

173
Good night David
no room for me
I sure miss playing.

174
M'm M'm good
those kind of sickos
I am so accurate.

175
You give up something
late Fridays
it's safer than candles.

Chapter 3

MILKING CONTEST

It enhances all natural juicy goodness
spend a few bills
I'd have to say apples

Here in Baltimore
a New York based artist

You're my lawyer
this is chicken kabobs
with people from all over the country
to prevent our next guest

You Bush league no talent
he passes the fastest fingers question
favorite sandwich
ball team

My program, you eat lots of food
pay the bills, and we go out

So what are we going to do
it's actually good for him

Mary Steenburgen
grilling machine
nations of foods
he ain't lying
the pitch.

I'm better than you are
I was amazed at the difference

Lori
without John Denver
looking for fun

The coverage continues

Straightener
the little engine that couldn't
all right
we have someone on the phone

I want to see that one
detangle, defrizz
ready for some hot action
two or three pounds a week
it's the biggest in the world

New revelations
cup and comb

For eighty-eight years
food
some fat person
until I saw
by check.

Softer

Hi mom

Now you can enjoy
the world's largest
actors and models

Don't miss this

When it comes to foreplay
grand ballroom
free three month supply

What do you mean
discover
the right answer
you've been trying
as the rate goes up

The boy had learned a valuable lesson
the following program
let's not keep them waiting
I don't feed him
thank you very much

She's with the program
usually about 35 or 40
guys.

Time to hit the road
you know it happened
just doin' my job

Credit, forget it
weekdays at seven
smile on
all week long

You love him right

We're going to play right now
he's free to leave
you were his mother
call

Wow
the Gettysburg address
I must say
I had a couple of friends on the team

You're too fine for her
sweating, nausea
large hand-stretched
frozen
everything else
pure.

She wanted things

I'm surprised to see you
tune in
every day

We gave it a bigger extended cab
look for that rain

One soldier was killed
possible
about 6:10 they came out

Leave you breathless
live look
Baltimore's favorite

Cleaning

Great resumé
training camp
she's so precious
along for the ride
the casual wine
unlimited evenings

This selection won't last
what's going on
you were great.

Charlie Foos was born in Baltimore, Maryland in 1972. He received a Bachelors of Fine Arts from the Maryland Institute College of Art and a Masters of Fine Arts from Hunter College. He is a founding Member of the international contemporary art movement, *Des Derrières*. Mr. Foos is a doer of various things and his turn-ons include long walks on the beach and eating pizza.

colophon

Text set in Trade Gothic with Andale Mono,
Rockwell & ITC American Typewriter accents.
Typesetting by Ellie Ga with Matvei Yankelevich.
Cover design by the author.

Cover letterpressed by Breck Hostetter. This
edition of 500 copies was printed and bound by
McNaughton & Gunn.

brought to you by
Ugly Duckling Presse

for further information and a catalog of our titles
please visit www.uglyducklingpresse.org